Lost and Found

Lost and Found

Michael Gottlieb

Roof Books
New York

ISBN: 0-931824-08-8
Library of Congress Catalog Card No.: 2003096462

Grateful acknowledgement to the editors of *Fence* and *Big Allis*,
where some of this work originally appeared. "Careering Obloquy"
was originally published as a chapbook by Other Publications.

Cover photograph by Richard Cohen.

Author photograph by Alan Davies.

Roof Books are distributed by
Small Press Distribution
1341 Seventh Avenue
Berkeley, CA. 94710-1403.
Phone orders: 800-869-7553
www.spdbooks.org

State of the Arts This book was made possible, in part, with public funds from
the New York State Council on the Arts, a state agency.
NYSCA

ROOF BOOKS
are published by
Segue Foundation
303 East 8th Street
New York, NY 10009
www.roofbooks.com

Contents

ISSUE OF ERROR

1.

Bitten down to the quick.

There you are,
like nothing so much as an unclaimed lot
bought back by the house,
not having met your minimum.

So once more
we try to take you
past the on-end view,
to that level grade that always seems sunk
in some harrowing particulate.

It is like servicing a debt,
a personal guarantee,
something tendered in a note.

As if you had been emancipated,
but not by this court.

What we have here is a bona fide secondary market,

and all of this—
a sort of knocker's shop.

Our job here,
downstream of the era of good feeling,
is to assess your break-up value,

all the while keeping watch
for the inescapable conclusions,
as they arrive,

in spate.

2.

The bright line,
the candid snap,
the large detail,
the faltering isolate.

The way you were forever to be found
at the front of the house,
adorning the narthex.
A breathing lobby card.

"You are,
even now,
one of us."

An artlessly heartfelt dismissal
loitering near the one-sheet,

discarded
along with the rest of the sharps.

Clotted abeyances.
Nagging embrasures.

How many more of you
did you say
there are
back at home?

3.

The things we stipulate to,
we must, we think about them so much.

A disturbing display,
brought out on name days
and inauspicious anniversaries.

Regularly genuflecting,
haruspsicating the alarums.

The very date and time—

nearly whole,
havering,
had.

Having been given this long, til the twenty-fifth
to file our complaint,
and no later,

then stacked by the counter,
a kind of merchandising dump,

succumbing wearily
to all that which has been baled up.

This much
we've agreed
not to talk about.

What we deign to disdain
seeping inconsolably
into whatever it is
without which it is impossible
to see the night through.

4.

There are adults
in need of supervision.

With all that penned-up demand,

what is called for
is a simple palliative,

but whatever it is,
it will be nothing compared to what you have left behind.

It could have been even *more* better.

Like a warning delivered through the good offices
of some supernally disinterested surmise.

What we can rely on is
this agreeable corruption,
this cheerful hatred.

We aired them,

that's our job.

5.

"Certainly, I will advert to all that."

It is one of our more friable terms-of-art,

part and parcel of our custom and practice,

by such capitulations
you shall know us.

We draw back the bloody stump,
we drink deeply of the draught,
that's why we're here.

Espying
a godlet on the local, smoking openly.
And later, in
the mens toilets at the Arcadia stop,

in the back room,
with the regulars,

"Once I was new too."

So, for the whole company
it eventually becomes
part of our unique selling proposition,
a kind of refrain—

"Who takes home the trick?"

And what used to be worn so lightly,
a base delight,
transmuted into that mischievous wormwood.

6.

By popular acclaim
one of us has been elected

Outlier For Life.

On our chosen glide path,
making our puissant approach,

hexing the prey,

our passage
tangled in our own discomfits,

all of us so greatly relieved
by the back-dated mourning,

we've come to believe that, despite the prop-wash,
we'd apparently escaped
quite nearly unmussed.

So we had no trouble shorting
whatever was left of our residual,
demissable, dry-eyed pudeur,

leaving us entirely disarmed
in the face of just this sort of eventuality—

that is,
ourselves,
showing up.

7.

This is low.
This is beneath you.

The way we are obliged to straighten,
bind, foreshorten,
debraid,

yet another
soon-to-be-regretted
landfall.

That which keeps getting snared in the works,
its tail growing longer,

famously alighting,

returning inevitably to a place where the walls themselves
are furred
with what is left of
what even you say is
unworthy of you.

How much more terrible
must it be below?

In the very same way
so many of us end up saying,
"The proper study of mankind
is me."

8.

Stout denial, that is the
traditional remedy among my people.

We study the coordinated outfits,
the assemblages and accommodations
that are wheeled up when we seek to break with it all.

Waiting for the carousel,
the forfeit and the suborned.
The shy platform.
The water hazard.

Like the exercise of the Peak And End rule.

As if that union
wasn't always fated
trying to marry such poor passagework
to the inevitable breakage and peradventure.

We were once very good friends, you should know,
with our extremities.

Now, we have barely any ambit left.
We throw up like girls.

9.

"I have no one to thank but myself."

Unmanned,
despite the great intervallic leaps,
by that lever of sin
– if only a wish
not unlike an exaggerated startle response.

The towering passing notes,
like thunderheads crossing your brows.

A view-finder, that's what missing.
A tepid, anodyne exit.

"Either that ends, or this does."

A through-and-through.

We note, over there,
the not unsurprisingly,
all too-neighborly, patternation
in the splash areas.

This is the sentimental vest.

Those are the noble gases.

10.

Unerringly familiar locutions
which
exhaust your patience at last,

like a bed sit,
with the wash-up
piled in the sink.

"Most threateners don't act
and most actors don't threaten."

There is a certain jouissance attached
to this order of events,

it leads us to ruinous declamations,
like, "you know me,"

or, "There are always more
than one of you,

and you are not
always the best example."

11.

The most famous of the gaffes,
collected in a sort of casket.

An unjust pasting,
like an itinerant riposte
addressed to an inattentive second.

A kind of monstrance,
a sneering reliquary

careful working on the cover,
chased figures,
signs of handling,

bespeaking a longstanding mortification of the flesh.

In the end
you had to correct us for salt.

The way that the argument that one should be allowed,
once and for all,
to walk upright
is eventually shot full of holes.

12.

After what we so wanted to believe
was manful struggling,
a calibration finally emerged fine enough
to recognize
prostrate from abject.

When one finally receives directions,

and is required to disembark,

this is what can be carried away:

a grandfathered unit of measure,

a consent decree
for the rest of us,

a means,

an eschewing
worried back to its kernel.

The flames, fully involved.

Who would have thought
this could all so quickly redound upon us?

In lieu of,
always.

13.

A repeater.

What we did to ourselves
and do still.

Vocalizing forbearance:
"it is like I hardly hear it anymore."

It is not just another cumbrous panel,
or artless shrinkage,
or flailing sally,
it is *us.*

While I cannot remember much,
I know I must forgot this.

Down among the traffic pillars and smudge pots,
the darkened way stations,
blasted depots well-forgot

how you tilted your grimace,
your fingers dashing through your hair,
the way you said, "Enough."

The resignation in the countenance.

The orbits of the eyes.

That coffer dam.

Struck foolish, for the last time.

14.

Like a sewing suggestion,
located below the fold,
near the answers to the Jumble,

always trying so,
so top of mind,

like a place where we liked to weed,

there, thick upon the ground,
the sentinel symptoms.

What we can always put down
as a custodial death.

And, floating over from the carport,
some improvident expostulations, like

"You're three over the limit,"
or, "He's good for the swing."

And no one is to know
what you know, or where you go,

patrolling those agency-less marches.

15.

A goner,
saying hello to the big guns:

"Okay, this very well may be your trade dress,
I'll grant you that."

A device,
a standard,
a plummeting halyard,
something we can all feel
good about abandoning.

That despicable buoyancy.
I can't throw you over,
not for long, at least.

This must be the secret of your success:

unlimited substitutions
pronounced upon the hour,

hollowed-out foot-faults,

unaccompanied registers
schooled to respond without reply.

There's action.
There's inaction.
And there's miming inaction.

16.

A kind of risorgimento
of the unacknowledged.

If we are lucky,
always there's some sort of
agogic pause,
or accent.

We try to assure ourselves that those noises
we have no choice but to hear
every night

will be revealed eventually as no more than
the unexceptional shudders
of a stray architrave or pediment

unmoored somehow,
drifting away from
our familiar, amicably stabilized ruins,

and not

their heels ringing upon the treads,
their steps echoing in the courtyard
as they mount the stairwell
and approach our door

– those failed familiars and remorseless shades,

our ganged evasions.

17.

"No one can help you now,"

is an introduction that usually goes entirely unremarked.

To incline the dome.
What one once bowed to.

For so long depending upon the baited demise,
now reduced to milling about with the others.

Detuned stage-business.

Hand-prompts in broad daylight.

Canny adjournments.

And in this corner,
the hardy pretender:

"He's really not doing anything wrong."

18.

This is not a sprite,

that is not a daybed,

but those are
neutral spirits.

You, and your premium decay,

a mournful dinning seeping into the carriage,

the voices continuing to aver,
without much evidence,
that the likes of us never could have gained
unaided admittance here.

An appreciated hope,
we try
to breathe life into.

It is risible
in its sorry dimensions.
and its thralldom

a galvanic, "I don't care."

Here lies the extravagant deception.

It was a tonic.
We all thought so, we applied
it so liberally.

To wake up next to that,

wreathed in smiles
like those.

19.

What appears to us,
the Great Incurious,
like nothing so much as a vanquished array,
a spoiled table,

like a dead hand upon the market,

in fact,
a piteously thin coat of pastiche.

Where what we thought we'd thrown away,
all that was to have been drawn down,
those felted impulses,
packed with gamy protestations,

were to be finally discharged, discounted
- so many cents on the dollar.

Addressing the funnel.

Appeals to another out-group.

An array of facile pivots.

Avouching for the irresolution.

The fond mould.

20.

None of us any the wiser.

And here you are, walking already,

nearly steady upon your pins,

despite what anyone else would have called
those confiscatory rates,

what else is there we can admit is
amiss?

Warning shots
one thinks are well deserved.

A flag of convenience.

A smash-up of unspecified, unmistakable origin.

This is the end
of the chin music

put down your dukes.

THE DUST

ONE

UHF Tower Mast A

VHF Main Antenna Bracing, Southeast

Left Rear Wheel Assembly, Retractor

Radome Array

First Class Galley Convection Oven Number One

First Class Galley Convection Oven Number Two

Knoll workstation fabric panel, 3'6" by 2', with crepe

Knoll workstation fabric panel, 3'6" by 2'6", with crepe

Knoll workstation fabric panel, 3'6" by 3'6", with crepe

BPI workstation 1/2 plexiglass panel, 5'6" by 2'6"

Hon workstation 1/2 plexiglass panel, 5'6" by 3'

Interior Concepts workstation T-base for non-raceway panels

Anderson Hickey workstation connector post, 6'

Global workstation full plexiglass panel, 5' by 2'6"

Seagrave Fire Apparatus Rear Mount Aerial Truck

Seagrave Fire Apparatus Tractor Drawn Aerial Truck

Seagrave Fire Apparatus High Pressure Pumper

Ford Crown Victoria Interceptor

Kroll-O'Gara Cadillac Fleetwood

Boucle short-sleeve shirt

Pigment-dyed oxford shirt

Stretch poplin shirt

Egyptian 60s long sleeve, barrel cuff, wing collar shirt

Merino V-neck sweater

Stretch plain-weave pleated pant

Stretch twill pant

Denim pant

Five button jean

Argyle broadcloth boxer

Looney Tunes characters broadcloth boxer

Distressed corduroy baseball cap

Flat black belt

Woven brown belt

Form F-3MEF New registration statement filed under
Rule 462(b) to add securities to a prior related registration
statement filed on Form F-3

Form U-9C-3 Quarterly report concerning energy and
gas-related companies pursuant to Rule 58 of the Act

Form S-6 Registration statement for unit investment trusts

Form N-8B-4 Registration statement for face-amount certificate

Frito-Lay Ruffles Original, 12 1/2 oz

Ben And Jerrys, Cherry Garcia, one pint

Snapple Peach Diet Iced Tea, 12 oz

Lifesavers Butter Rum, economy pack

Altoids, cinnamon, 1.76 oz

Twizzlers Nibs Licorice Bits, 2.25 oz.

Camel Light 100s, hard box

Lancome Revitalizing Cream

Revlon Fantastic Blusher

Chanel Age Delay Rejuvenation serum

Clinique Pretty Long Lashes mascara

Estee Lauder Multi-Dimension powder

Ortho Novum, Dispensa-A-Pak

Tampax lite days

Flonase 50 mcg

Lescol, 25 mg

Column tree connector

End plate and top

Rail 3/8" by 6' by 12'

Fillet weld 3/8" by 6'

Flange connection

Stiffener

Spandrel

Carver Rectangular Genuine Wood Wastebasket

Post-it "Important" Note Pad, Assorted Neon Colors,
50 Sheet Pad

Sanford Liquid Accent Tank-Style Highlighter, Orange

Avery E-Z D Ring Heavy-Duty View Binder with
Lever-Lock, Black

Hewlett-Packard Color LaserJet 4550 Laser Printer

Swingline Full-Strip Desktop Stapler, Black

Acme Forged Steel Scissors with Black Enamel Handles

Bic SoftFeel Ballpoint Stic Pen, Black

Charmant green frame, number 4435

Eyespace, wire frame, Model A222

Luxottica, 6678m

Titmus Optical, Safety Indoor/Outdoor

Transitions, Extreme Twist Frame

National Gypsum Board Number Four

National Gypsum Board Number Six

Pittsburgh Plate Glass

Shield, Port Authority of New York and New Jersey Police, Chief Of Department

Shield, Court Officer, Supreme Court Of New York

Global Deluxe Task Chair with Height Adjustable Arms, Blue

Lifetime Lightweight Folding Table, 29" by 30-1/2" by 72", Stone gray

Sauder Camden County Executive Desk, Planked Cherry Finish

O'Sullivan 5-Shelf Heavy-Duty Bookcase, Snow

Bush Cubix Collection 36" Desk, Medium Cherry/Slate Gray

Office Designs Commercial 26-1/2" Deep Vertical File Cabinet, Putty

Hon 600 Series 30" Wide 2-Drawer Lateral File, Black

Cisco 3600 T1/Ft1 CSU/DSU Module

Cisco 2621 Ethernet Router 2 10/100 Ports 2 Slots
3com Superstack 3 Modular Switch 3300 24-Port 10/100

D-Link Systems DSS— 24 Plus Rackmount 24 Port Switch

Bay Networks Business Policy Switch 2000 Auto 24

3com Deh5695 Switch 4005 Fan Assembly

The Wall Street Journal

The Financial Times

The Economist

The Straits Times

The Far East Economic Review

The Hollywood Reporter

SteelWeek

Milliken Carpet, 32 oz nylon level stitch

Collins and Aikman, 28oz 60/40 nylon/olefin blend

Ductwork— Single Wall Round

Ductwork— Double Wall Round

Ductwork— Single Wall Oval

Stretch multitwist slash blouse

Cotton three-quarter sleeve blouse

Silk cashmere fine-rib V-neck blouse

Stretch merino striped blouse

Silk herringbone dress

Silk charmeuse printed dress

Floral print silk dress

Cotton/Lycra demi underwire bra

Cotton/Lycra full figure underwire bra

Lace-trim mesh bikini

Vine floral-printed panty

Single ankle-strap shoe

Brown front-band sandal

Black ankle-wrap flat

Assignment of Mortgage— Individual Mortgagee/Holder

Petition for Temporary Restraining Order and Permanent Injunction

Statutory form of Quitclaim deed for corporation to execute. State of New York

Nonqualified Stock Option Agreement of N(2)H(2), Inc. granted to Eric H. Posner dated September 30, 1999

Sprint PCS Kyocera 2035

Sanyo SCP-4700

LG Touchpoint TP1100 PCS phone

Sprint Samsung SPH-N200

Motorola V2397EPW

Blancpain Flyback Chronograph

Swatch Mickey Mouse Fiftieth Anniversary Commemorative

Seiko Automatic 24, Model L334

Engagement ring, Tiffany setting, platinum, three-point
four carat diamond

Mikimoto cultured pearls, double strand, white gold clasp

Helmet, New York Fire Department, Firefighter, Ladder 4

Helmet, New York Fire Department, Chief, Second Battalion

Bunker Coat, New York Fire Department, First Deputy
Commissioner

Bank One Visa Gold

Chase MasterCard

New Jersey Department Of Motor Vehicles, Operators License

Commonwealth of Massachusetts, Drivers License
Passport, United Kingdom

Employee Identification, Risk Waters Inc.

Employee Identification, Fred Alger Management

Employee Identification, Summit Security Services

USAirways Dividend Miles, membership card

National Association Of Broadcast Employees & Technicians,
Communications Workers of America, Local 16, membership card

City University Of New York, Baruch College, Student
Identification

Little League Baseball, New York District 20, Hastings On Hudson,
Umpire Registry Identification Card

Joseph P. Kellett

Joseph J. Keller

Peter Kellerman

Frederick H. Kelley

Joseph A. Kelly

Maurice Patrick Kelly

Timothy C. Kelly

Thomas Kelly

Thomas Michael Kelly

Thomas W. Kelly

Richard John Kelly, Jr.

TWO

Seton Identification Products, 30339V, "Emergency Exit Only Alarm Will Sound"

Avaya Merlin 34 button Deluxe BIS-D telephone set, with 6' handset cord

Myst III: Exile, for Windows 98, CD-ROM, Ubi Soft Entertainment, Inc.

Johnson & Johnson Band-Aid Brand Adhesive Bandage, 1/2" by 3"

Picture Frames By Umbra, Fits Pictures 3 1/2 by 5

Daniel C. Lewin

C++ For Dummies, Stephen Randy Davis, 4th Edition, IDG Books

Lite Source, Inc. portable lamp, Model BF51520

Totes Automatic collapsible umbrella, Black

Fisher Price "See N Say" Baby Says

John J. Tipping, II

At-A-Glance Reversible Erasable Wall Calendar, 36" by 24"

Instinet Russell 1000 Reconstitution Preview— update, pdf

Bordeaux, La Fleur, Petrus, 1998, 750 ml

Alysia Basmajian

Orchid, Cattleya Leopoldii

Kwikset Titan key

Michael Quilty

Alban Berg's Wozzeck, The Metropolitan Opera, September 26, 2001, Orchestra, AA110, AA111

Julio Minto Balanca

Rollerblade, ABEC X10 Extenblade

Kiran Reddy Gopu

John Patrick Salamone

Hartmann 44" Overnight Lite Garment Bag

Ching Ping Tung

Sushil Solanki

Lyudmila Ksido

Coffee, regular, sesame bagel, toasted with cream cheese

Jorge Luis Morron Garcia

Kathy Nancy Mazza-Delosh

Jayceryll M. de Chavez

Jimmy Nevill Storey

Quarter, two dimes, two nickels, three pennies

Raymond M. Downey

George Eric Smith

Oscar Nesbitt

CAREERING OBLOQUOY

1. Spinning Up

This smiling resemblance, this is what they dub it—

attended by a mute, iatrogenic demurral at every step.

We have been studying ruination for so long
that a kind of constructive disavowal, like a shot across the bows,
has finally come to redound upon us,

at this place where burn permits
are issued freely,

like refusal simple,

or unassayed samples,

and defiance is sent
to all the crazed finishes.

The way, over the years, we come to resemble our clay.

I wish I still had it,
that certificate of destruction.

2. With The Safe And Loft Squad

Behind the party wall, over by the de-monetized lots,
the unchecked papering continues,
up and down the street.

We did mean to be more careful,

as if we knew no better than to believe
there was a difference between
"thinking about you" and "thinking of you."

False swearing is another name for it,

as it debouches into a larger way,

almost a thorofare,
a kind of defile,

and here is the stain upon the sidewalk.

It's been here for years,

What we end up with instead of a commemorative marker.

3. A Wrecker And A Splittist

Hellebore brooking no argument,
all of a sodden piece,

that's why he got here first.

Astride the harbor are found the fighting words,
they can just be made out,
penned with that trademark frank duplicity,

all the storm-melt,
and the second-guessed masking,

another incident packed with moment.

The way we used to take for granted
the quiet enjoyment of these premises.

There's a furious decay in the slurry,
sealed with that shaking hand—
it's bought up,
we bring it up.

And yet,
we abide not.
Flailing in like manner,
we have come to resemble him.

Here on the burning plains
no one paid any less attention to him
than they did to anyone else.

Dangling from the tines, a fully formed man,
gesticulating meaningly.
We can just hear him.

4. Version Control

This too can be borne.
We are all of bearing age.

And because there is no *unlike,* all are alike, except for you.

This used to be a parlor of a sort,
a place where people parlayed,

a locus of an unaccountable urge to avoid,

where there was always more to be said—
what you lost, who gained thereby—
and how sorry were we all.

You can draw your own conclusions.
It's a story we're good at telling.

There was once a marshalling yard hereabouts,
vast arms stretched into the yawning, fretful dusk,
some practiced disorder in the three-point recessionals.

I hear the coughing still.

It is a noise that carries.

5. Strum, Drone And Build

We have not quite gone missing,

but to participate in a fighting retreat like this,
that's something I should never have asked of you.

Those lonely, terrifying gifts.
The hall of disclaimers.
A kind of hectoring.
The sapping contretemps.
Greedy trepanning.
To remember that distemper.
Mildew— our recompense,
and here, the unsavory mote.

As we regroup at somewhat more defensible lines,
the question arises,
what do we have to show for ourselves,

besides this definition of *apartment*—
looking at all the space
that resides between us all . . .

how do we keep the churn rate
from falling further?

All of that hand-eye coordination, we need it now.

6. The Mercy Rule

We are the walking proof.

Themes and practices
not uncloyingly
erode inevitably into roles and responsibilities,

like mortality, a kind of haring, not a chase,
another routine, as opposed to morbidity.

The issue of this union, all too often contested,
flees pell-mell from us.
And who wouldn't?

We've been kept on retainer
for just these sorts of opportunities.

Regaling ourselves with that appealing trace
of fusty peradventure,

calamities, not challenges,

while our friend Doreen, the most irenic of spectators,
who has no alternative but to follow along in the right of way,
finally arrives at her pied-à-terre
at the Distrait Arms.

The damning scent,
all that was left.

What we came to call Life Drawing.

7. This Page Intentionally Left Blank

You come to believe you can "collect them all,"

it is like throwing blows,
a kind of weather,
a flurry of affect,
fronting dismay,
leveraging the affright,
broadcasting wholesale distraction,
tumbled for the relict,
sewn-in welts.

As if that part of you which can never get clean
was somehow made up,
cut from whole cloth,

a kind of wash and wear,

as a poor choice of words precedes us down the stairwell,

to a place where we all must attend— this viewing,
this careful muggery, this fragile carapace.

I take from you,
and so do you,
and you,

no less incurious than any of us.

Discovering only now that there is no moiety after all,
as we find ourselves in those jolting chairs, once again.

8. Your Pull Date

The tidy and the particulates.

How much smaller may we dice you?

It's the coating, a therapeutic misadventure in fine,
a static of palliatives laid, course upon course,

so many tell-tale adjournments
and hasty replantings,

a fakebook
writ large—

and scrawled across its strato-cumulous,
this much we do not know.

It is more than we usually have in hand, at the end,
as it empties into the resigned estuary:

a blistering consolidation,
a topical reagent,
a gainsaying treatment,
a subdural reply,
an asymmetric lump.

Unit histories, the asides of scullions and lint folders,
shy, reticulos, squamos,

interposed countersignatures, pilled suites.

The retired colors.

9. Taunting, Shaming, Shunning, Slander

She was the cosine of error within us,

and we were the tables she ran,

as she got shirty with the group,
mapping the proposition, muttering under her breath,
"this is a good place for a battle."

There is a regnant principle,
among the line-breaks,

whether one likes it or not,

so that what we end up saying,
what remains in the filter after screening,
the decloaking actors in whose success we've invested so much,
those steadfast irresponsibilities—
where would we be without them?

The felon's progress.

A four-color plate of Buyers Remorse.

10. Wearing Its Ignorance Lightly

This is the second lamp of architecture
and here is the dark fiber
where I light you up with my connivance.

We looked out upon the intersection
and the early graves and late, where we visit you,

where we're always playing ourselves, but badly,

as if one could be surprised by the speed at which
the denials you thought you knew,
had let your guard down to,
suddenly all went into a kind of syndication,
and in some way now were replicable in an orderly but
not entirely predictable progression.

That is what always surprises us— the way we fall for it,
again and again,

that awful insiderism,

like a lengthy recovery which is prescribed,

what they used to call a bed cure.

Exercising a certain ascendancy.

All of a sudden, seeing us all as just more special pleading,
and that was not enough.

11. Our Joint Communiqués

Our armamentarium— our lack of arguments,

you don't need to put in the hours, this is not production work.
In fact, it is far preferable not to have enough time
for this sort of thing.

Amour propre splayed across the page.

Vagrant troughs.
Teary among the welcome hallos.
A bracelet of distraction.
Baled up indictments.
The dutiful perforation.
Artful foot-faults.
Withal. Overweighted. Plenum. Jouissance.
Surgical staples.
Weedy queuing.

A voided space— too small for a closet,
from it wafting a nacreous aroma,
what we call the new diffidence:

"I couldn't care less."

So we end up asking, "Would you mind taking this quiz?"

And then, later,
"How many more of you did you say there are back at home?"

12. Breakfast In Kind

The cockpit of resignation,
where we exercise the right of free passage.

All that's left around here— what I have left to put in play—
this monstrous gaze.

There was a time when all it smacked so of the uncanny.

The way that a precept like this
could be plated and deposited in front of us
as if it was nothing less than
the serving suggestion for today.

Part of why this proposition is so compelling
is that it never shows any dirt,

only a few minute travails,
a kind of insulation,
wrapped like puttees with a feigned cunning.

Think of me as a sort of
temporary filling,

and all this as a kind of campaign, say,
a regimen of something we might call
direct inaction.

13. In The Service Of

As we gather in the Ascending Rooms,

we've somehow decided this was sufficient,

we've enough go to market with—

a bygone imposture,
a hissing gauge,
a pending defalcation,
a good poke

- that's all that's usually called for.

"I do not do much.
It is my shame.
But this much,
I will not do for you."

That beckoning, benevolent virus inside us all—

like an imposture of authorial cramp,

all that craven rewriting.

14. The Hypothecated

I stood along with the rest
but I did not applaud,

waiting so long in the cold before finally realizing
that this too was a kind of decision tree.

Now I see that while I have straight-line responsibility here,
yours is a dotted line.

"It's not that I think that I am different than you.
I just think I'm better than you."

As if suddenly we had agreed to let everyone use a pencil.
Not just a pencil, but an eraser too.

And for that moment
we were no longer proctors,
we were just like everyone else,

prey to that narcissism of small differences

which could always get you ejected from the premises—

theft of services.

15. Unified Messaging

What we discard in the early hands,
which later, it never quite seems worth attaching a name to,
nevertheless, throwing a sediment,
and so, we score it anew, and we will do so, perpetually.

A shade, a miscue, an attenuated guy-line.

The way that revising and restating my bad trades quite nearly,
and quite often,
absolves me of all of your successes.

This descending staircase— *"what I want of you . . . "*
and where I'll go to find it,

how much I'll pay, and what I've gainsaid already,
how much I'm short,
the horrors that we eventually come to visit upon them,
one and all.

This pier of favor, this acceding failure to submit,
this jerry-rigged foreshortening,
this successor-in-interest.

I saw you in the dark bar.
There were capital requirements.
It was nothing personal.

This blind gall that argues on,
that would otherwise have been sussed out,

but now sits in its morning shambles, half revealed—
"Go, get decent," we want to say.

16. Note To Self

We all have to wait our turn for the lukewarm appointment
and that less-than-bracing topper—

"Please play again."

What everyone wants to know,
but just not right now, is

how many months did we end up spending upon those stairs,
counting the door, operating without cover,
losing heart at full cry,

casting glances at the bulk loaders, skirting the docks,
heading up-river
toward the towering elevators?

This is where I messed.
This was my pup tent and my broom.
Here, my flashlight.

As if you were a tonic we needed to apply liberally to the misdeed.

We will not enjoy good health.
We will not be surrounded by luxury.

As we maneuver to *the reveal*,
we have to.

17. Careering Obloquy

What we answer to now—
a mere pipette.

As the accommodating array of options
becomes a wasting disease, like any other,

it becomes clear that there's no graceful rejoinder,
no distance learning,
no moving sidewalk.

While you're not old quite enough to be in the way,
you're still invisible,
and I am reduced by this care—

in the welcoming barrens, alongside the fumbling megrims,
while we've been distracted
an eerily preserved turn-signal has been unearthed,

as the last, best of them all
is remanded yet again to another authority . . .

a visiting power,
a deflationary regime,
some piled-on, hazy tolerances

. . . to a place where excuses, like initials,
are carved into the warp.

And the contending scapegraces,
like so many plowed-under back-formations—
try to stand to, still,
as sentinel.

But we have ways of making you
shut up.

ROOF BOOKS

- Andrews, Bruce. **EX WHY ZEE**. 112p. $10.95.
- Andrews, Bruce. **Getting Ready To Have Been Frightened**. 116p. $7.50.
- Benson, Steve. **Blue Book**. Copub. with The Figures. 250p. $12.50
- Bernstein, Charles. **Islets/Irritations**. 112p. $9.95.
- Bernstein, Charles (editor). **The Politics of Poetic Form**. 246p. $12.95; cloth $21.95.
- Brossard, Nicole. **Picture Theory**. 188p. $11.95.
- Champion, Miles. **Three Bell Zero**. 72p. $10.95.
- Child, Abigail. **Scatter Matrix**. 79p. $9.95.
- Davies, Alan. **Active 24 Hours**. 100p. $5.
- Davies, Alan. **Signage**. 184p. $11.
- Davies, Alan. **Rave**. 64p. $7.95.
- Day, Jean. **A Young Recruit**. 58p. $6.
- Di Palma, Ray. **Motion of the Cypher**. 112p. $10.95.
- Di Palma, Ray. **Raik**. 100p. $9.95.
- Doris, Stacy. **Kildare**. 104p. $9.95.
- Dreyer, Lynne. **The White Museum**. 80p. $6.
- Edwards, Ken. **Good Science**. 80p. $9.95.
- Eigner, Larry. **Areas Lights Heights**. 182p. $12, $22 (cloth).
- Gizzi, Michael. **Continental Harmonies**. 92p. $8.95.
- Goldman, Judith. **Vocoder**. 96p. $11.95.
- Gottlieb, Michael. **Ninety-Six Tears**. 88p. $5.
- Gottlieb, Michael. **Gorgeous Plunge**. 96p. $11.95.
- Greenwald, Ted. **Jumping the Line**. 120p. $12.95.
- Grenier, Robert. **A Day at the Beach**. 80p. $6.
- Grosman, Ernesto. **The XULReader: An Anthology of Argentine Poetry (1981–1996)**. 167p. $14.95.
- Hills, Henry. **Making Money**. 72p. $7.50. VHS videotape $24.95.
  Book & tape $29.95.
- Huang Yunte. **SHI: A Radical Reading of Chinese Poetry**. 76p. $9.95
- Hunt, Erica. **Local History**. 80 p. $9.95.
- Kuszai, Joel (editor) **poetics@**, 192 p. $13.95.
- Inman, P. **Criss Cross**. 64 p. $7.95.
- Inman, P. **Red Shift**. 64p. $6.
- Lazer, Hank. **Doublespace**. 192 p. $12.
- Lazer, Hank. **Doublespace**. 192 p. $12.
- Levy, Andrew. **Paper Head Last Lyrics**. 112 p. $11.95.
- Mac Low, Jackson. **Representative Works: 1938–1985**. 360p. $12.95, $18.95 (cloth).
- Mac Low, Jackson. **Twenties**. 112p. $8.95.
- Moriarty, Laura. **Rondeaux**. 107p. $8.
- Neilson, Melanie. **Civil Noir**. 96p. $8.95.
- Pearson, Ted. **Planetary Gear**. 72p. $8.95.

ROOF BOOKS
are published by
Segue Foundation, 303 East 8th Street, New York, NY 10009
Visit our website at **segue.org**

ROOF BOOKS are distributed by
SMALL PRESS DISTRIBUTION
1341 Seventh Avenue, Berkeley, CA. 94710-1403.
Phone orders: 800-869-7553
spdbooks.org